MacDonald

by John Mackay

LangSyne
PUBLISHING
WRITING *to* REMEMBER

Lang**Syne**

PUBLISHING

WRITING *to* REMEMBER

79 Main Street, Newtongrange,
Midlothian EH22 4NA
Tel: 0131 344 0414   Fax: 0845 075 6085
E-mail: info@lang-syne.co.uk
www.langsyneshop.co.uk

Design by Dorothy Meikle
Printed by Ricoh Print Scotland
© Lang Syne Publishers Ltd 2014

ISBN 978-1-85217-054-7

MacDonald

SEPT NAMES INCLUDE:

Beaton

Beith

Bowie

Connall

Darroch

Donald

Donaldson

Gilbride

Galbraith

Gerrie

Gowrie

Hewison

Houston

Hutcheson

Johnson

Kellie

Kinnell

Kinniburgh

MacBride

MacConnell

MacCutheon

MacGeachie

MacEachern

MacHugh

MacIan

MacIllwraith

MacKelloch

MacRory

May

Murchison

O'May

Purcell

Revie

Shannon

MacDonald

MOTTO:
By Sea and By Land.

CREST:
From a Coronet, a Hand in Armour
Holding a Red Cross Crosslet.

TERRITORY:
The Western Isles
and the West Highlands.

Chapter one:

The origins of the clan system

by Rennie McOwan

The original Scottish clans of the Highlands and the great families of the Lowlands and Borders were gatherings of families, relatives, allies and neighbours for mutual protection against rivals or invaders.

Scotland experienced invasion from the Vikings, the Romans and English armies from the south. The Norman invasion of what is now England also had an influence on land-holding in Scotland. Some of these invaders stayed on and in time became 'Scottish'.

The word clan derives from the Gaelic language term 'clann', meaning children, and it was first used many centuries ago as communities were formed around tribal lands in glens and mountain fastnesses.

The format of clans changed over the centuries, but at its best the chief and his family held the land on behalf of all, like trustees, and the ordinary clansmen and women believed they had a blood relationship with the founder of their clan.

There were two way duties and obligations. An inadequate chief could be deposed and replaced by someone of greater ability.

Clan people had an immense pride in race. Their relationship with the chief was like adult children to a father and they had a real dignity.

The concept of clanship is very old and a more feudal notion of authority gradually crept in.

Pictland, for instance, was divided into seven principalities ruled by feudal leaders who were the strongest and most charismatic leaders of their particular groups.

By the sixth century the 'British' kingdoms of Strathclyde, Lothian and Celtic Dalriada (Argyll) had emerged and Scotland, as one nation, began to take shape in the time of King Kenneth MacAlpin.

Some chiefs claimed descent from ancient kings which may not have been accurate in every case.

By the twelfth and thirteenth centuries the clans and families were more strongly brought under the central control of Scottish monarchs.

Lands were awarded and administered more and more under royal favour, yet the power of the area clan chiefs was still very great.

The long wars to ensure Scotland's

*"The spirit of the clan means much
to thousands of people"*

independence against the expansionist ideas of English monarchs extended the influence of some clans and reduced the lands of others.

Those who supported Scotland's greatest king, Robert the Bruce, were awarded the territories of the families who had opposed his claim to the Scottish throne.

In the Scottish Borders country – the notorious Debatable Lands – the great families built up a ferocious reputation for providing warlike men accustomed to raiding into England and occasionally fighting one another.

Chiefs had the power to dispense justice and to confiscate lands and clan warfare produced a society where martial virtues – courage, hardiness, tenacity – were greatly admired.

Gradually the relationship between the clans and the Crown became strained as Scottish monarchs became more orientated to life in the Lowlands and, on occasion, towards England.

The Highland clans spoke a different language, Gaelic, whereas the language of Lowland Scotland and the court was Scots and in more modern times, English.

Highlanders dressed differently, had different

customs, and their wild mountain land sometimes seemed almost foreign to people living in the Lowlands.

It must be emphasised that Gaelic culture was very rich and story-telling, poetry, piping, the clarsach (harp) and other music all flourished and were greatly respected.

Highland culture was different from other parts of Scotland but it was not inferior or less sophisticated.

Central Government, whether in London or Edinburgh, sometimes saw the Gaelic clans as a challenge to their authority and some sent expeditions into the Highlands and west to crush the power of the Lords of the Isles.

Nevertheless, when the eighteenth century Jacobite Risings came along the cause of the Stuarts was mainly supported by Highland clans.

The word Jacobite comes from the Latin for James – Jacobus. The Jacobites wanted to restore the exiled Stuarts to the throne of Britain.

The monarchies of Scotland and England became one in 1603 when King James VI of Scotland (1st of England) gained the English throne after Queen Elizabeth died.

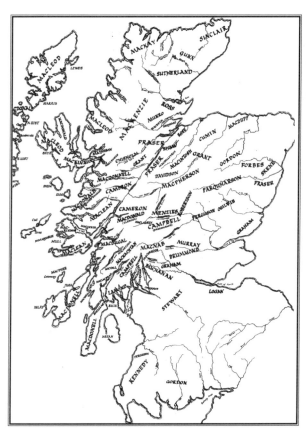

A map of the clans' homelands

The Union of Parliaments of Scotland and England, the Treaty of Union, took place in 1707.

Some Highland clans, of course, and Lowland families opposed the Jacobites and supported the incoming Hanoverians.

After the Jacobite cause finally went down at Culloden in 1746 a kind of ethnic cleansing took place. The power of the chiefs was curtailed. Tartan and the pipes were banned in law.

Many emigrated, some because they wanted to, some because they were evicted by force. In addition, many Highlanders left for the cities of the south to seek work.

Many of the clan lands became home to sheep and deer shooting estates.

But the warlike traditions of the clans and the great Lowland and Border families lived on, with their descendants fighting bravely for freedom in two world wars.

Remember the men from whence you came, says the Gaelic proverb, and to that could be added the role of many heroic women.

The spirit of the clan, of having roots, whether Highland or Lowland, means much to thousands of people.

Chapter two:

Men of war

The MacDonalds have their ancestors in the renowned Lords of the Isles who viewed themselves as laws unto themselves outwith the rule of the sovereign on the mainland.

They held the Western Isles in an iron grip and their territories extended as far south as the Isle of Man. They also became earls of Ross and were the great rivals of the Campbells of Argyll.

One of their heroes was the mighty and ferocious warrior, Somerled, who fought the Norsemen (carrying off and marrying Eric the Red's daughter) before being slain by the Scottish king Malcolm IV in 1164.

One of his grandsons, Donald, gave his name to the whole clan ("Mac" meaning in Scots 'the son of') and their loyalties were divided during the Wars of Independence with most of them supporting Robert the Bruce and prospering accordingly.

Visitors to Scotland incline to picture the Highlander of old as a man solely of the heather-clad mountains but the MacDonalds, as with other clans based to the west, were also seamen. In the late 16th century rhythmic oars under a square sail were still roving the Hebridean seas as they had done since the days of the Vikings and many were the stories told of the rovers' prowess.

For instance, the Mackenzies received reports of a MacDonald fleet of over 30 galleys having set out to harry the coast of their lands; and a woman gathering shellfish near Applecross told of a "great galley" which had recently disappeared round an arm of the land nearby. The Mackenzie boat was sent in pursuit while fighting men sped overland, catching the MacDonald galley by surprise and in the ensuing fight killing their enemy's leader.

Angus, the leader of the MacDonalds, vowed revenge and planned a naval engagement for the coming Spring. Mackenzie also prepared for battle and from his headquarters at Eilean Donan Castle sent out a call to other friendly clans for support. Lady Mackenzie gave her followers two brass cannon, lead and gunpowder.

The battle early in the following year was fought bitterly for days and even at times in the moonlight. Angus was among the casualties and did not recover. Lady Mackenzie arranged a funeral appropriate for such an honoured foe. After such a bloodletting and the result inconclusive with both sides having fought themselves to a standstill it merely led to further raids and vendettas in the years ahead until the MacDonalds by sheer numbers got the upper hand.

In the 1300s Robert the Bruce had granted lands of Lochaber to Angus Og of the Isles in recognition of the part played by the MacDonalds at the battle of Bannockburn but later their claim to these lands were disputed by rival clans and they had to fight tooth and nail to hold onto them.

But the MacDonalds also had territorial ambitions of their own and on one memorable occasion sailed galleys up Loch Ness to storm Urquhart Castle.

The MacDonalds were also involved in constant running battles and ambushes with Royalist forces keen to impose the shackles of centralised government on them.

On one occasion King James 1st had Alasdair MacDonald kidnapped and imprisoned in a dungeon in Tantallon Castle on steep cliffs overlooking the Firth of Forth, east of North Berwick, about as far away from the chieftain's followers that it was possible to get while still staying in Scotland.

But Alasdair's men continued their fight

against the King's men and a cousin of his led a successful attack against a Royalist regiment garrisoned at Inverlochy Castle. As a section of the MacDonalds advanced on the castle, another group sailed south then cut back overland into a position in the braes above Inverlochy where two hundred bowmen poured arrows into the enemy.

After the Royalist defeat, Alasdair was grudgingly released with the condition that he punish his men who had taken part in the raid on Inverlochy, something he singularly failed to do, claiming they had fled to Ireland (as some indeed had). As a result his lands were confiscated by the Government and Alasdair kept up a vigorous but vain lifelong campaign to win them back.

Chapter three:

Headhunting

Eventually, the clan had their lands returned to them and little is heard of the chiefs until the 10th, also called Alasdair, appeared on the scene at the beginning of the 17th century.

This Alasdair was a man of some culture, well educated and who in his college days in the south was a fellow student with a Macfarlane of Luss on Loch Lomondside.

Later they would visit each other as part of the social scene – yet the broadsword was never left long enough in its scabbard to rust.

A fugitive Highlander appeared at a house owned by a MacDonald laird, asking for food and shelter for his men of the clan Gregor hiding nearby from Argyle's warriors. He was refused and the laird sent a message to Keppoch Castle, Alasdair's stronghold, informing his chief who surprised the Gregors in their hiding place and killed them. He sent their heads to Edinburgh and was rewarded with a grant of £100.

Alasdair and Macfarlane in their student days had ventured abroad and, of all social graces, had been shown conjuring tricks and later performed displays for their clansfolk.

Some of the audience feared they were witnessing the works of the Devil, while others were full of admiration and called their chief 'Alasdair nan Cleas' (Alexander of the Tricks).

On a sojourn down south, Alasdair was entertained by an English baron who boasted of his silver plate adorning the dining table and of the superbly fashioned candlesticks illuminating the scene, remarking that his guest in his Highland fastness could not match the display.

In time the baron came north and visited Keppoch and when he was shown into the ancient banqueting hall was surprised at the dramatic spectacle of twelve Highlanders ranged in full warrior dress round the room, each holding aloft torches of flaming pine.

"These," his lord observed, "are MY priceless candlesticks which all the wealth in England cannot buy!"

In the winter of 1644 King Charles I was on the throne and much troubled by the Covenanters. The Royal army in Scotland with the Marquis of Montrose as Captain General and Alasdair ('young Colkitto'), the son of MacDonald of Colonsay as Lieutenant General, opposed Campbell of Argyle's forces.

Montrose and his men headed for Inverness to win support and on reaching Fort Augustus on their way up the Great Glen had word that Argyle's men were laying waste to the Lochaber lands in revenge for Montrose's plundering of Campbell territory.

After a forced 30 mile march over the snowy mountain vastness, Montrose led his 2000 men on a vast outflanking movement, taking his enemies totally by surprise. With the MacDonalds in the front line advancing to the wild music from their great Highland bagpipes, the Royal Army swept Argyle's men from the field.

News of Campbell's force had been given by one of the extraordinary characters in this story who had then led Montrose through the mountains – Iain Lom of the Donald clan, a famed Gaelic bard. It was said that before the battle began he was offered a sword to take part in the attack but refused, saying that his part was to record what would be a famous victory and this resulted in a notable Gaelic epic poem.

Around 1500 of Argyle's Campbells had been killed and their chieftan let it be known that he would give a handsome reward to anyone who would bring him the head of the man who he considered the initial cause of the defeat – Iain Lom.

Some time later a stranger called at Argyle's home at Inverlochy and said that he had come for the reward.

"Where," asked the chief, "is the head?"

"Here!" was the answer and the stranger pointed at his own head for it was Iain Lom himself.

Argyle was so amused at the nerve of the man that vindictiveness gave way to admiration for such a character and Iain became an honoured guest at Inverlochy for several days – without further mention of heads.

Chapter four:

Young blood

In the 1680s Archibald of Keppoch, the 15th chief, was succeeded by his son Coll, a teenage student at St. Andrews University, who had to leave his studies to take over the clan affairs at home.

He visited Inverness, hoping to settle an ancient feud with the Mackintoshes whose answer to that friendly approach was to have young Coll imprisoned in the Tollbooth. The Marquis of Huntly, a friend of Coll's, contacted the Privy Council who ordered the young chief to be set free. Coll, his overtures of friendship having been roughly spurned, now decided on the opposite course and got support from the MacDonalds of Glenshee and Glengarry. The battle that followed was the last to be fought between clans in the Highlands with victory going to the MacDonalds.

An Inverness lad who had run away to fight for the Mackintoshes later wrote:

"We were no sooner in order but there appeared double our number of the MacDonalds who came down the hill without either shoes, stockings or bonnets. They broke in upon us with sword, target and Lochaber axes which obliged us to give way. Having never witnessed the like before, I was sadly affrighted and ran many miles before I looked behind me."

Since the Mackintoshes has been augmented with government redcoats, the MacDonalds thought it prudent to return to their mountain fastness, only to see soldiers firing their homes and burning their ripening harvests.

Another milestone in the clan's history came when a young chief, Alasdair Glas, was murdered by a jealous cousin. On taking over, the 14th chief failed to condemn this murder. Iain Lom, however, swore that he would see justice was done, no matter how rough it might be, and with the help of Sir James MacDonald a body of 50 fighting men assembled on the Brae of Lochaber and led by Iain came to the home of a cousin who was slain along with six of his relatives who had been part of the murder gang.

The heads of the murderers were cut off and washed by a spring at the side of Loch Oich. The heads were presented to Lord MacDonald of Invergarry Castle and then taken to Edinburgh where they 'were affixit on the gallows'.

The site where the heads had been cleaned is

marked today by a stone monument known as 'The Well of the Heads', the column of the monument being surmounted by the seven heads carved in stone.

In 1689 Cameron of Lochiel asked Coll to bring his men to Inverness to meet Viscount Dundee, the Jacobite leader, and to escort him into the Highlands in an attempt to win the support of clansmen living in the remoter areas.

En route to Inverness, Coll and his fighting force wreaked vengeance on the Mackintoshes and their associated clans by fire and plunder through the Great Glen; and on arriving before Inverness, Coll, now a seasoned warrior, demanded a ransom from the magistrates against the possibility of his men ransacking the town. He also requested a jacket of scarlet and gold fashioned for himself.

For three days Coll bargained with the officials then Viscount Dundee arrived and condemned the MacDonalds' action but was careful to ensure he still had the support of his clansmen and later on Skye Coll was made Lieutenant Colonel of a regiment raised by Sir Donald MacDonald.

During the ensuing campaigns, Dundee gave the title of 'Coll of the Cows' to the chieftan since the Viscount had noticed that, when rations were low and meat on the hoof ahead had been driven into the mountains well away from the advancing army, Coll seemed always to successfully search them out.

Coll died in the 1730s, according to a poem recording his notable life, and one of the last of his ventures involved joining, along with his son Alasdair who became the 17th chief, in the Jacobite Rising of 1715. An important date in the clan's history was 1691 when the Government announced there would be pardons for past misdemeanours to all the clans who "made their submission" to the Crown before the last day of the year. Coll decided to comply and get on the right side of the law for once thus saving his people from the fate of the MacDonalds of Glencoe.

One point on the infamous massacre is clear – high authority in the person of the Master of Stair relished the fact that Glencoe had not managed to take the oath of allegience by 1st January, 1692. In his communication to the King, Stair wrote:

'It will be a proper vindication of public justice to extirpate that sept of thieves and it must be quietly done, otherwise they will make shift for both men and their cattle. Let it be secret and sudden.'

Chiefs who had been loyal to James VII were

offered a pardon by King William if they swore the oath. At such time the weather worsened, beginning to play its part in the tragedy. On the last day of 1691, the ageing chief Alasdair of Glencoe arrived in Fort William where the governor, who had been the means of persuading some clans to take the oath, refused to take Glencoe's, explaining that the chief would have to go to Inveraray, and gave him a letter to the sheriff there asking him to accept Glencoe's submission.

Old Alasdair arrived in Iveraray on January 2nd but had to wait there until the 5th of the month before the sheriff, a Campbell, appeared. He agreed to observe MacDonald's taking of the oath but explained that since this had been done after the appointed date this would have to be reported for consideration by the Privy Council in Edinburgh. This typical example of an exalted authority in action is matched by the following note in a diary of that time, "If the Glencoe men could be separated from the rest of the Highlands some example might be made of them in order to strike terror into the rest."

The delays forced on MacDonald in his attempts to conform suited the King who signed an order to make the MacDonalds 'an example'. He probably never even read it through for the diary again quotes, 'He was too apt to sign papers in a hurry without examining the importance of them'.

The question of why a section of an Argyll regiment should be stationed in Glencoe at the beginning of February was not initially explained to the commanding officer on the ground. Apparently he was content to obey orders and he and his men fraternised with the MacDonalds and were given Highland hospitality until on the 12th the order arrived that the MacDonalds were to be annihilated – 'You are to have special care that the old fox and his sons do on no account escape your hands. You are to secure all the avenues, that no man escape'.

At five o'clock next morning the slaughter began. Glencoe was transformed into a winter hell where snows reflected the lurid flames from the burning clachans. The screaming of the dying and bellowing cattle being driven from their sheds, the yelling of the soldiers, the crackle of musketry – all added to the terror invading the glen.

The chief was shot in the back as he struggled to get out of bed. His wife was robbed of her jewellery and sexually assaulted. Yet more died of exposure in that awful place as they fled from the scene than were killed by the sword or gun.

Few in authority emerged from the outrage with credit. One who did so was Sir John Lauder, Lord Fountainhall, a Member of Parliament for Haddington who, offered the post of King's Advocate, refused the honour when he was told that one of the conditions of his accepting was that he should not prosecute those implicated in the Massacre.

Chapter five:

Rebellion

The MacDonalds were prominent supporters of Bonnie Prince Charlie during the 1745 Jacobite Rebellion. It was Ranald MacDonald, chief of Clanranald, who met the Prince when he landed at Moidart. At the battle of Prestonpans they formed the right wing and swarmed down on the Government troops in the early morning mists, yelling their ancient war cries and whirling their claymores savagely and mercilessly.

At the battle of Culloden in 1746 the clan chief Alasdair was wounded and as he was carried from the blood-soaked moor passed a lad trying to rescue his wounded father who, when he saw his chief, made his son leave him and join the men helping Alasdair to a hut away from the carnage. It was hoped he could be hidden from the Duke of Cumberland's vengeful troopers while his wounds could be dressed but by the time he reached shelter he had died.

The MacDonalds of the Brae of Lochaber were the last to lay down their arms and say their farewells to the Prince prior to his boarding a French ship at Borrowdale so the clan had been there at the beginning and at the end of the doomed rebellion and been very active in between.

And the most famous MacDonald of them all played her part in the Prince's escape.

Flora MacDonald was born on South Uist in 1722. The daughter of a laird, she was educated at a boarding school in Edinburgh where she learned all the cultured arts of the time, becoming expert at music in particular. Her skills on the small pianoforte and harp meant that she was in much demand in the drawing rooms of the great and the good.

She stayed at the house of her clan leaders, Lady Margaret MacDonald of Skye and her husband Sir Alexander of the Isles, in Edinburgh when the first rumours of the Rebellion started.

Returning to the Hebrides, Flora followed the progress of the Jacobites avidly, being sympathetic to their cause. When the Prince became a fugitive after Culloden, the islands were invaded by hundreds of redcoats looking for him and a price was put on his head.

Word was passed to Flora that Charles was sheltering in a cave on South Uist and it was decided to transport him to Skye where he might have a slim chance of getting aboard a French ship.

It was Flora's stepfather, Captain Hugh MacDonald of Armadale, who hit on the idea of having his attractive 24-year-old stepdaughter take the Prince, disguised as Betty Burke, an Irish spinning maid, across the sea to Skye.

Flora first met the Prince in a small hut where she helped him change into the petticoat, gown, apron, cloak and hood gathered from the wardrobe of Lady Clanranald, which was now to be the costume of Betty Burke.

Needing all her courage and calmness, she went with her 'maid' to a small boat and in pouring rain and pitch darkness they set off through the patrolling ships and a wild thunderstorm towards Skye.

Skirting the shoreline, they were fired on by some Highland militia but kept their heads down and rowed to safety round a headland.

When it was found that the 'safe' house where they had planned to take the Prince was swarming with troops, Flora calmly walked in and after some idle socialising managed to get some food and wine for Charles who was hiding in a cave.

The following day she coolly made her way along a dozen miles of tracks with her 'maid' past Government troops to the house of a sympathiser where the Prince was given warm food and his first sleep in a bed since Culloden.

Now dressed as a Highlander, the Prince, along with Flora, made his way to Portree where they parted company after she had entrusted him to the Jacobite MacLeods of Raasay. The Prince had tears in his eyes as he grasped his saviour's hands and bade her a tender and affectionate farewell, disappearing into the darkness and the rain.

The role of Flora was crucial in his escape. Without her help it is extremely doubtful if he could have avoided the clutches of the Government troops who were rapidly closing in on him. He was trapped on the island and it was only a matter of time before he would be discovered.

When the authorities learned of Flora's role in Charles's escape, she was taken to London where she was kept in prison for a year.

But an Act of Indemnity was passed which freed her and she was permitted to return home (the Government shrewdly had no wish to make a martyr of her).

She married in 1750 and her husband was the son of Alexander MacDonald of Kingsburgh. The couple emigrated to America and in 1775 Flora's husband Allan joined the Royal Highland Emigrant Regiment on the side of the British in the War of Independence. They were imprisoned after a string of rebel victories.

Flora had in all seven children – five sons (who all became army officers) and two daughters – and in 1779 she was allowed to sail home. Her husband was eventually allowed to join her and they lived quietly in Skye.

Flora died in 1790 and she was shrouded in one of the sheets in which the Young Pretender had slept on Skye, a relic she had religiously carried with her in all her travels.

She was buried at Kilmuir and the cortege was more than a mile in length. A dozen pipers played a lament.

She lies next to her husband and a tall Celtic cross looms above the grave on which are inscribed the words:

'A name that will be mentioned in history, and if courage and fidelity be virtues, mentioned with honour.'